Ripley Hitchcock

Etching in America

Ripley Hitchcock

Etching in America

ISBN/EAN: 9783337164614

Printed in Europe, USA, Canada, Australia, Japan

Cover: Foto ©Thomas Meinert / pixelio.de

More available books at **www.hansebooks.com**

The first plate Etched in the New York Etching Club

ETCHING IN AMERICA

*WITH LISTS OF AMERICAN ETCHERS AND
NOTABLE COLLECTIONS OF PRINTS*

BY

J. R. W. HITCHCOCK

NEW YORK
WHITE, STOKES, & ALLEN
1886

NOTE

IN CONNECTION WITH THE FRONTISPIECE.

THREE of the organizers of the club shared in the preparation of the first etching of the New York Etching Club. The "ground" was laid by Mr. James D. Smillie, Mr. R. Swain Gifford drew the design, and Dr. Leroy Milton Yale "manned the press" and took off the first impression. This was on an evening in the winter of 1877–78, when some twenty artists, more than half unacquainted with the process, met in an up-town studio to organize an etching club and to gain some practical knowledge. In the preface to the first illustrated catalogue issued by the club, Mr. James D. Smillie has described the etching of the frontispiece-plate as follows: "Those twenty interested artists formed an impatient circle, and hurried through the forms of an organization, anxious for the commencement of the real work of the evening. Copper plates were displayed; grounds were laid (that is, delicate coatings of resinous wax were spread upon the plates); etchings were made (that is, designs were scratched with fine points, or needles, through such grounds upon the copper); trays of mordant bubbled (that is, the acid corroded the metal exposed by the scratched lines, the surface elsewhere being protected from such action by the wax ground), to the discomfort of noses, the eager wearers of which were crowding and craning to see the work in progress. This process being completed, in cleansing the wax grounds and varnish from the plates the fumes of turpentine succeeded those of acid. Then an elegant brother, who had dined out early in the evening, laid aside his broadcloth, rolled up the spotless linen of his sleeves, and became for the time an enthusiastic printer. The smear of thick, pasty ink was deftly rubbed into the lines just corroded, and as deftly cleansed from the polished surface; the damped sheet of thin, silky Japan paper was spread upon the gently warmed plate; the heavy steel roller of the printing-press, with its triple facing of thick, soft blanket, was slowly rolled over it, and in another moment, finding scant room in the pressing crowd, the first-born of the New York Etching Club was being tenderly passed from hand to hand."

PREFACE.

THERE are histories of American painting and engraving, but "Etching in America" is the first book devoted to this branch of our art. As a history, it records the subserviency of etching in the hands of our early engraver etchers, and the various influences leading to the late emancipation of etching as an art. There is included, my introduction to "Recent American Etchings," published last year by the publishers of this volume. But, aside from mere historical narration, it has seemed essential that something should be said against a style of etching which, while retrogressive in methods and commercial in motive, yet meets with a certain degree of popular favor. On the other hand, I have tried to do full justice to our artist etchers, and by the citation of examples I have hoped to direct a larger share of public attention to the consideration of work intrinsically valuable. A plea for the persistent recognition and maintenance of pure painters' etching, and a frank analysis of the rapidly developed demand for etchings, have seemed to me much needed at the present time. Some account is given of the growth of American print collecting, and of the present private and public collections; but, for the most part, I have confined myself to American etching.

For this an apology is not needed. The connoisseur can consult Bartsch, Dumesnil, Passavant, Weigel, Thausing, Dutuit, and the whole army of continental writers of general works or of critical biographies and catalogues. For the ordinary print-lover, there are Hamerton's "Etching and Etchers," Maberley's "Print Collector," and Bryan's "Dictionary of Painters and Engravers." Technical processes are not dwelt upon in this volume because, beyond the now familiar elementary process of drawing designs upon a grounded plate, and biting the lines into the copper with acid, technical methods are of little interest to the general reader. The etcher on the other hand would hardly thank a layman for instruction, which he can obtain at first hand from Hamerton, and from the hand-books of Lalanne, Martial and others. With all this material within reach, to say nothing of the new " Print Collector " promised by M. Eugene Dutuit, and the weighty volume upon etching lately published by Mr. S. R. Koehler, who has done much to advance the best interests of the art in this country, it has seemed only judicious to restrict myself so far as possible to ground which has not been covered before. This little book is not intended to be exhaustive. If it be found suggestive, the author's chief purpose will be satisfied.

My thanks are due to Messrs. James D. Smillie, Henry F. Sewall, Frederick Keppel & Co., and S. P. Avery, for many kindly offices. I have also to acknowledge the courtesy of Mr. R. Swain Gifford, and Dr. Leroy Milton Yale, who have generously permitted the use of the plate from which the frontispiece is printed. It need hardly be said that this plate, which was etched merely to illustrate the process in a company including many novices, is not to be taken as representative of Mr. Gifford's work. It is peculiarly interesting, however, on account of its history and associations, and it is used because the first plate etched by the oldest and strongest etching club in this country, which has been, and is, the centre of our etching, seemed to me to furnish the most fitting frontispiece for a volume upon "Etching in America."

J. Ripley W. Hitchcock.

New York, February, 1886.

ETCHING IN AMERICA.

THE etching is no longer confounded with the pen-and-ink sketch or the drawing upon lithographer's stone. Needle, ground, plate, and mordant are terms used as glibly in our current vocabulary as references to brush, mahl-stick, palette, and canvas. There are few of us so poor as to lack some general knowledge of the art. There are few so bold as to refuse to do reverence to the etching. In these days of enthusiasm it is taken rather as a compliment than otherwise to be reminded that popular interest in the art is hardly six years old in this country. This fact we accept as proof of our quick intuitions, and we pride ourselves upon our uncommon powers of appreciation. Etching is our youngest art, and in view of its youth an attempt at a biography may seem at present premature. And yet the height of chalcographic enthusiasm which we have so suddenly reached is an excellent point of observation. On the one side is the work of our early engraver-etchers, succeeded by the elevation of etching from its fallen state of servitude to supremacy among the linear arts. On the other, there are signs of a growing tendency among etchers to ignore free-hand painter's etching and to be influenced by popular demand into a style of elaborated work which differs little from the engraver's etching of our fathers. We can watch the pendulum through its arc and see at least the beginning of its returning swing. As regards popular taste, the etching fever is emerging from the violent stage to enter, let us hope, a healthier period of convalescence. Altogether, American etching, despite its youth, has already become an interesting study, and it is the more interesting from its variety, which offers so many exceptions to any general characterization. It is impossible to dispose of American etchers in a phrase or two, when only ten of the number show such individual work and divergent methods as are seen in a recently published collection.

There is an incongruity in alluding to an art which has existed, and at times flourished, for three hundred years, as if it were born yesterday. Yet the existence of etching has always been fitful and uncertain. According to Mr. Hamerton there was nothing to be compared with the school of Rembrandt until the school of Flameng arose in the present century. All this time etching was practised to some extent in Europe, and the American artists of the last century who went abroad must have had some acquaintance with the art, although the acquaintance never ripened into friendship. Etching here, as in England, was first employed by engravers simply as a means of forwarding work which was finished with the burin, and even with the ruling-machine. In any history of line engraving there will be frequent references to the employment of etching. Gerard Audran, who led the so-called classical Renaissance school in the latter half of the seventeenth century, was accustomed to hasten his work by the use of etching, and the English engravers of the last century sometimes substituted the needle for the burin. In this century mixed methods have been extremely prevalent. Mr. Hamerton instances modern engravings, after Rosa Bonheur, by H. T. Ryall, C. G. Lewis, and T. Landseer, in which "the tone of the skies is got by machine-ruling, and so is much undertone in the landscape; the fur of the animals is all etched, and so are the foreground plants, the real burin work being used sparingly where most favorable to texture. Even in the exquisite engravings, after Turner, by Cooke, Goodall, Wallis, Miller, and Willmore, the engravers have recourse to etching, finishing with the burin and dry point." These accounts of mixed methods may seem superfluous to engravers or to etchers, but they are necessary for a layman's comprehension of the allusions to etching which appear in the early history of American art.

Take, for example, that curious old volume of William Dunlap's, "History of the Arts of Design in the United States," a singularly minute portrayal of the straits to which our early artists were too frequently reduced. Nearly fifty years ago Dunlap wrote: "Engraving or working with the graver was the first or oldest practice. Etching followed and became an auxiliary to the engraver." An auxiliary indeed! Only a few years ago Dr. Haden was among us, uplifting the art of etching and casting stones at the mechanical trade of engraving. Now that the disciples of Hamerton and Lalanne are everywhere, poor old Dunlap's definitions would be promptly ruled out of any court, and yet he correctly formulated the practice of his times. In fact, even in these days the needle and burin are associated oftener than is dreamed of by the average admirer of the etching. Is the pendulum swinging backward? But for the present let us confine ourselves to Dunlap. He mentions Peter R. Maverick, originally a silversmith, who "etched and engraved for many years in New York. In 1787-88," writes Dunlap, "he taught me the theory and practice of etching, and in his workshop I etched a frontispiece for a dramatic trifle then published. He had his press in his workshop." Now, Maverick was a mechanical engraver, and while he could teach Dunlap how to lay a ground, mix his mordant, and bite his plate, the instruction could not have gone beyond engraver's etching. Dunlap, to be sure, was a painter, but it is improbable that he executed a free-hand etching without assistance from the engraver's tools. The same can be said regarding the work of other engravers mentioned in this volume. There was Alexander Lawson, a native of Scotland, who came to this country in the latter part of the eighteenth century. After some use of the graver, Lawson "had points made for etching and tried that. I then got a mezzotinto tool and tried that mode of engraving. I tried everything, and did nothing well for want of a little instruction." Lawson was reduced to finding employment as an engraver with Thackara & Valance of Philadelphia. "Their art consisted in copying, in a dry, stiff manner, with a graver, the plates for the Encyclopædia, all their attempts at etching having miscarried.

They also engraved card-plates, dog-collars, door-plates," etc. From this it appears that Lawson appreciated the distinction between etching and mechanical engraving better than some of his contemporaries. Evidently he had an ambition to take up etching as an art, but his hopes were frustrated. Our early art history abounds in records of ambition brought to naught by the bitter necessity of bread-winning in uncongenial but immediately remunerative pursuits. In mezzotint engraving Lawson was anticipated by Jennings, who came from England about the beginning of the Revolution, and, according to Dunlap, executed "probably the first mezzotint scraped in America." This was from a portrait by Copley of Nathaniel Hurd, who divides with Paul Revere the honor of being the first American engraver. Of Francis Kearny, 1780-1804, Dunlap says: "Drawing he studied under Mr. Archibald Robertson and his brother Alexander. Line engraving, etching, aqua-tinto, stippling, and soft-ground etching were all studied by the young engraver, principally by the aid of books." It was an engraver, not an etcher, who struggled to teach himself these various arts in the absence of any facilities for art education. Could Thackeray, when he depicted the travels and experiences of Michael Angelo Titmarsh, ever have heard of John Rubens Smith? An artist of this name lived in New York about 1812. He "both etched and scraped in mezzo-tints. His design and etching of George Frederick Cooke's monument, erected by Kean to the memory of his predecessor, in St. Paul's

Churchyard, New York, with the figures of Kean and Dr. Francis, had some notoriety at the time, and more in England since Kean's death." But John Rubens Smith, I fear, regarded etching only as "an auxiliary to engraving."

Now the painter's etching, a freehand drawing upon a grounded plate, autographic in character, expressing the individuality of the artist in lines directed by the immediate brain-impulse of the man, suggestive rather than elaborated, is obviously a very different thing from the engraver's etching, in which the needle is but one of half-a-dozen tools, and the biting one of several processes, of which the printing is by no means the least important. It may be said that this definition of engraver's etching applies to many etchings of the present day. True, but we have not yet followed the pendulum through its arc. No one of those whom I have mentioned can be called the first American etcher, meaning, of course, a painter-etcher. This honor is to be awarded, on the authority of Mr. W. S. Baker, to Joseph Wright, son of Patience Wright, a modeller in wax, who was born at Bordentown, N. J., in 1756. He was one of the few artists of that time who enjoyed an opportunity of studying in London and Paris. As the story goes, the first American etching was a portrait of the George Washington whom most of us know as a demi-god rather than as a man. In the winter of 1790, Washington was a regular attendant at Trinity Chapel, New York. Thither also repaired the artist Wright, but not to pray. The sermon fell upon deaf ears, for Wright, armed with crayon and paper, passed the time of service in drawing a profile portrait of Washington, quite without the knowledge of his involuntary sitter. From this crayon drawing he made an etching which Mr. Baker calls "probably the first ever executed by a painter in this country." The statement in this form is incorrect, for Dunlap gives 1787 as the date of his own experiments with the needle. But Wright's etching may have been executed without adventitious aids, and it is probable that Dunlap employed the burin at least. This stolen portrait of Washington was printed on a small card and published the same year, and "in this shape," says Mr. Baker, "has come down to us, one of the most faithful and interesting portraits of Washington. It represents him in uniform, and was esteemed at the time to be an excellent likeness. The etching is executed with much taste and freedom, and became known in England shortly after its publication by close copies made by the engravers Collyer and Chapman." This portrait appears on the "Twigg Medal" and other pieces, described by Mr. Baker in his "Medallic Portraits of Washington." A needle first employed in tracing the lineaments of Washington should have been heard of afterward, but I know of no subsequent etchings by Wright. The claim put forth in his behalf is not beyond dispute; but I fancy no one will care to dispute it, nor to question this interesting tale. For one, I am quite ready to acknowledge Joseph Wright as the first American etcher, and the portrait of George Washington as our first simon-pure etching.

A few years later Robert W. Weir,

the first of a well-known family of artists, became interested in etching from paintings. He wrote Dunlap that "about 1820 I had copied some of Rembrandt's etchings so close as to be with difficulty detected, and was on the eve of turning my attention seriously to the publication of etchings from various old pictures in the possession of different gentlemen in New York, but like many other things of the kind it fell through after the first or second plate was finished." This was our earliest attempt at a systematic reproduction of paintings by means of the etching needle, a branch of the art without which the schools founded by Unger, Flameng, and Waltner would be of very much less consequence. But in this country etching from paintings by "old masters" has never flourished for lack of accessible material, and Mr.

J. S. King's serious efforts in this direction have been welcomed on account of their novelty as well as their sterling merit. In 1820 there was clearly no demand for this or any other application of etching beyond that made by the engravers, who held the art in their own hands until within the last generation. The old-time historical engraver used the graver altogether, the burin line being thought best adapted to the treatment of flesh, and much of the work of the old landscape engravers was governed by the most arbitrary conventions. Taking a small section of such engraving, with its lozenge and dot or square arrangement of lines, enlarging it and placing beside it an etching, the engraver's work naturally appears absurd. Obviously such a comparison is unfair, yet this is precisely what was done by

Mr. Haden when lecturing in this country. He succeeded in illustrating the superiority of the needle over the burin, but his comparison of a part of the engraving with a complete etching was imperfect, and, moreover, he gave the modern engraver slight credit for his knowledge and use of etching. Any one who has studied the best landscape work of our three veteran engravers still living — Messrs. Smillie,[1] Sartain, and Ritchie — will be inclined to modify some of Mr. Haden's conclusions. I have before me six states of an engraving by Mr. James Smillie, after a landscape by Asher B. Durand. The subject was first drawn on an etcher's plate and bitten in, the result being a slight sketch with an almost total absence of tones. Then a re-biting ground was laid. The darker lines were bitten again, and certain delicate lines were merely painted with acid. The burin was employed, and many of the lines re-worked in the effort to get the full line of tones in the painting. Then the sky and other flat tints were obtained by the use of the ruling-machine. These successive processes can be traced in the changing foliage, ground, water, and sky of the different states, until the final result is an engraving of surpassing mechanical nicety. Clearly the superiority of free-hand etching over such fine but labored work as this needs no demonstration, but at the same time the knowledge and rare skill shown in such landscape engraving should receive a fair recognition. If I seem to devote undue space to this point, it is because etching in America in the last generation was only represented by such work as this.

I have found etchings set down in catalogues of early Academy Exhibitions held nearly fifty years ago, and some of the older artists deem the distinction between etchings and engravings unimportant. Yet these Academic etchings no more deserved their name than did the engravings of Mr. Smillie. There was one work of this class which could be literally termed an etching. That was a projected engraving, after a painting of "The Landing of Columbus," which was to have been published by the old "Art Union" in the early fifties. The "Art Union" fell to pieces, and the plate never advanced beyond the etching state. A few impressions were taken in this state, however, and these, of course, may be called etchings, although they only serve to illustrate the use made of the art by engravers.

It was about this time that two American painters began to interest themselves in etching. One—Mr. George L. Brown—executed nine etchings in Rome between 1853 and 1855, which were published here in 1860. Mr. Brown, who was without special technical training, was actuated by a desire for artistic effects, but his work was influenced by the conventional methods of his time. Mr. J. G. Chapman, who spent the greater part of his life in Rome, is spoken of as an etcher of considerable manual delicacy, but as mechanically proficient rather than creative. Contemporary with these artists was a Mr. Burt, who etched many paintings in miniature, the copies usually intended for catalogues. More important work than this was done by Mr. Edwin White and Mr. J. M. Falconer. The former, better known as an historical painter of the last generation than as an etcher, died in 1877, but Mr. Falconer lives to contribute yearly to the Exhibitions of the New York Etching Club. If not the oldest of our etchers, he is among the first in order of seniority. Etching was then an indeterminate phrase, as was proved by its application to prints from outline drawings by Mr. F. O. C. Darley upon lithographer's stone. These colored prints were published as etchings by the old "American Art Union." But the engraver and lithographer were not to be alone in their appropriation of etching. The photographer was to put in his claim. Several years later, Mr. John W. Ehninger invented a process in which the design was drawn upon a plate of glass coated with chemically pure silver, the coating as easily removable as the wax ground on an etcher's plate. The glass was placed against black velvet and photographed upon sensitive albumenized paper, the drawing, of course, showing perfectly black. By this method "etchings" were made from pictures by Kensett, Durand, Casilear, and others. Some of them I have at hand. They are slight, not unpleasant little sketches, suggestive of the camera, and not at all of the etching-needle. I believe Mr. Ehninger found that etchings could be printed from the plate after the usual treatment at less expense than by his process. Of late years a way has been discovered of photographing a pen-and-ink sketch upon a plate covered with a specially prepared ground. When the transferred drawing is in readiness, the lines are bitten in as usual. An etching called "The Modern Etcher," exhibited by Mr. Robert Blum in 1883, was prepared in this way, and in the catalogue of that Exhibition there was an etching by Mr. J. C. Nicoll, which had been reduced by the aid of photography, something, of course, not at all uncommon.

The experiments of Messrs. Ehninger and Darley possess only a curious interest, and the introduction of soft-ground French engraver's etchings, which appeared here as early as 1845, is not to be looked upon as exercising any significant influence. As we know, the modern revival of true etching began hardly thirty years ago in France, and less than twenty years since in England. Mr. S. P. Avery, who has made a singularly fine collection of modern etchings, has proofs from plates etched by Calame, the Swiss painter, as far back as 1838. In 1844 an English etching club, including among its members Cope, Redgrave, Cheswick, and Frederick Taylor, issued a portfolio, entitled "Etched Thoughts," which was followed by "Songs of Shakspere," and other publications. Such instances were exceptional at the time. Even twenty-five years ago etching was only a recreation with those French and English artists who practised this art at all. They etched for sheer love of the work, frequently scraping off their plates and beginning on another subject without dreaming of publication. It was in 1853 that Léopold Flameng appeared in Paris, where he was destined to found a famous school. It is hard to think of a modern etcher who has exercised a wider influence. Flameng trained some of the most skilful etchers of the day, certainly the best reproductive etchers of our time. Yet popular appreciation was slow in coming. Mr. Avery tells me that when he visited Paris in 1867, he found the etchings of Jacque and Daubigny lying unsold in shops on the quay, although the price was only a franc or a franc and a half. Desiring to obtain a complete set of Daubigny's etchings, Mr. Avery visited the artist, who selected fifty proofs and signed them. When the question of price arose, Daubigny remarked that the proofs were exceptionally good, and he thought them worth fully a franc, about nineteen cents, apiece. Even the etchings of Méryon, that strange original genius, went begging in company with the work of Delacroix, Millet, and Jacque. Chauvel was then a lithographer. Fortuny in these years was busying himself with etching, and his influence subsequently became an important factor in the development of the art.

Up to the later sixties, therefore, etching had gained little hold upon the general public abroad or upon the artists in this country. But about this time an eloquent evangelist began to preach the gospel of the etching line in England, and the French public began to be affected by the efforts of the energetic publisher A. Cadart. I think it hardly possible to overestimate the effect of Mr. Hamerton's writings. In January, 1866, he published an article upon etching in the *Fine Arts Quarterly Review*, and in 1868 appeared the first edition of his "Etching and Etchers." I deem it no exaggeration to say that the modern revival of etching has been due very largely to this book. Mr. Hamerton interested the public as well as artists, and he gave an unprecedented value to the work of some men who had received little general recognition, like Mr. Haden and Mr. Whistler. On the other side of the Channel, M. Cadart not only published etchings and endeavored to make them popular, but helped to organize a *Société des Aqua-Fortistes*, and essayed a black-and-white conquest of America. In 1866 an exhibition of French etchings and some paintings was held at No. 625 Broadway, New York, under the directorship of M. Cadart. This gave the general public and a majority of our artists their first opportunity to see a collection of modern painters' etchings. M. Cadart brought into a rather feeble existence an American branch of the French Society of Etchers. Messrs. Victor Nehlig and Edwin Forbes were among the earliest members, and Mr. Forbes etched one or two plates for the Society. Some ten years afterward he was elected to membership in the old London Etching Club. His war etchings, called "Life Studies of the Great Army," were published soon after the Cadart exhibition, and a set of the first proofs was purchased by General Sherman for the War Department. I believe that Mr. Forbes merely drew his design on the grounded plates, leaving the biting and printing to others. The plates were heavily inked, and the printing unattended by the refinements first mastered by Paris publishers. Thus etching gained a foothold here. Mr. Hamerton's "Etcher's Hand-book," Lalanne's treatise on etching, and the introduction of modern French etchings by various dealers, strengthened the interest aroused by the exhibition of M. Cadart. Messrs. Avery, J. W. Bouton, and others furnished some examples of Jacque, Daubigny, Jacquemart, Fortuny, Appian, Rajon, and their brethren. Mr. F. B. Patterson, who began to deal in portfolios of French etchings soon after the Cadart exhibition, secured plates and etcher's tools and endeavored to interest such artists as Mr. E. A. Abbey and Mr. C. S. Reinhart. Much of the print business of fifteen years ago was in the hands of Nassau Street booksellers, who gave especial attention to extra illustrating books for their patrons. But by degrees print collectors began to look for modern etchings, and a demand arose which, among other results, caused the graduation of Mr. Frederick Keppel from a down-town bookstore to rooms where the modern French work was honored with a place beside early prints. Thus, early in the seventies, English literature and French art, with the etchings of Mr. Haden and Mr. Whistler, had begun to teach our public that the etching was a desirable acquaintance; and our artists, seeing that the work of their French brethren was well received, fell to considering whether they should not go and do likewise. The sowing of seed was nearly at an end, and the harvest time at hand.

One of the first fruits of the new influence was a series of etched views of old New York by Mr. Henry Farrer, one of the earliest and most persistent of our present etchers. His records of our picturesque and antique buildings were gathered into a portfolio issued by Mr. Patterson about 1872.

Perhaps half-a-dozen other American artists were etching with more or less regularity, but they were stimulated rather by a fondness for the art and the appreciation of their friends than by the existence of a general market. Mr. A. W. Warren, who left New York some fifteen years ago, to become the Instructor in Art at Annapolis, used both to etch and to advocate the organization of an Etching Club even at that early date. In later years some of Mr. Warren's etchings were reprinted, and with more intelligent printing they lost their hard, dry appearance, and took on almost a new character, an experience shared by some of Mr. Whistler's earlier work. Mr. Warren, I believe, did not live to see the foundation of the Etching Society which he suggested. The etchings shown at our Centennial Exhibition, which aroused a new interest in every form of art, may have been the immediate stimulus to the organization of the New York Etching Club. This was effected in 1877, with Dr. Leroy M. Yale as the first president. Of the twenty artists who met in response to the call, "more than half knew absolutely nothing about the most elementary of the processes." Mr. Smillie, whose well-stored memory, accurate knowledge, and collection of prints have been placed at my service with generous courtesy, had etched plates for several years before the organization of this Club, and was intimately acquainted with the technical mysteries of the art. I have seen etchings by Mr. Peter Moran, published as far back as 1876; and two New York amateurs—Dr. Leroy M. Yale and Mr. J. F. Sabin—with Messrs. R. Swain Gifford and F. S. Church, may be counted among the earlier proselytes.[2] Mrs. M. N. Moran, Messrs. Thomas Moran, Kruseman van Elten, and Samuel Colman were among the early members of the Etching Club. Mr. Stephen Parrish, who is popularly held to be a veteran, first published an etching, "Old Barn, Chester County, Pa.," in 1879, and Mr. Pennell's first work was of an even later date, as was his membership in the New York Etching Club. In the first three years of the Club's existence over one hundred and twenty plates were etched by members and discussed at the meetings. For two years—from 1879 to 1881—selected etchings by members were published in the *American Art Review*. This was the first introduction to our public of an association of American etchers. In 1881 an exhibition of American etchings was held at the Boston Museum of Fine Arts. This included several engraver's etchings, dating back for nearly half a century, for it was intended to illustrate the history of the art in this country in addition to presenting examples of modern work. Meanwhile our etchers were receiving encouraging recognition across the sea. In May, 1881, the first exhibition of the "Society of Painter-Etchers," organized by Mr. Haden, was held in London. American etchers had been asked to contribute. Some accepted the invitation, and cordial and intelligent appreciation of their work was accompanied by the election of several to membership in the new Society. These were Mrs. M. N. Moran and Messrs. James D. Smillie, R. Swain Gifford, Henry Farrer, Thomas Moran, J. M. Falconer, A. F. Bellows, Stephen Parrish, F. S. Church, and F. Duveneck. Other Americans—Mr. Pennell, for example—were elected afterward. In 1882 the New York Etching Club held its first formal exhibition and began the publication of an illustrated catalogue. Toward the close of the same year the Philadelphia Society of Etchers held its first exhibition, which was enriched by selections of prints from the collections of Mr. James L. Claghorn. Interest in etchings grew apace, stimulated still further by Mr. Haden's lectures in the winter of 1882–83. Any personal expression of his views was probably unfamiliar to the majority of those who were acquainted with his etchings, although in 1878 Mr. Haden had published a treatise, "About Etching," which consisted of notes upon a collection of his own exhibited in London. In this country Mr. Haden found artists and collectors who were able to meet him upon the common ground of an intelligent and critical interest in the art. That he did something toward placing painter-etching in its true light before our public there can be no doubt. On some points he was controverted, but the presence of an etcher strong enough to provoke lively discussion was thoroughly beneficial.

Anything like a *catalogue raisonné* of our present etchers is impossible within these modest limits. Over sixty American etchers contributed to the last exhibition of the New York Etching Club. Exhibitions of etchings are yearly held in several of our larger cities, and tidings of the formation of etching clubs come to us even from beyond the Canadian line. Professional men dabble in the art, and reduce staid households to a state of inkiness and despair. The gentler sex has abundantly disproved Hood's lines on "Needlework Art," which run—

> "It scarce seems a ladylike art that begins
> With a scratching, and ends with a biting."

And yet, with all this devotion to the art, it cannot be said that we have a distinctive American school of etching. No one has as yet arisen among us strong enough to wield such an influence as Flameng has exercised in France, or Unger in Germany, or Haden in England, to say nothing of the inspiration derived from Jacquemart, Méryon, Fortuny, Whistler, and Waltner, although Waltner has become a professional copyist. Our etching is of a composite character, showing traces of both French and English influence. Storm van s Gravesande, the delightful Belgian etcher, whose collected works were exhibited in New York last winter, has probably aided in training some of our etchers, and others have been affected by Unger and his school. Messrs. Smillie, Gifford, Pennell, Bacher, Dr. Yale, and at least two members of the Moran family, are among those who have used the etching-needle in sketching directly from nature. Within the last year or two reproductive etching in America has risen to a place of no little importance. American etchings after the old masters are rare, but the interpretation of American paintings by etchers like Messrs. Hamilton Hamilton, S. J. Ferris, Thomas Moran, Stephen Parrish, Thomas Hovenden, Walter Shirlaw, and others, is becoming familiar to our public. The announcement that Mr. Thomas Moran has etched a large plate after Mr. Harry Chase's "Fishing Boats at Anchor," or that Mr. Hovenden is engaged upon an etching after his painting, "The Last Days of John Brown," excites no particular comment in these days, but only a few years ago it would have met with unintelligent wonder. In spite of the influence of the French etchers, notably, perhaps, Fortuny, I think that Mr. Haden has exercised a stronger personal influence upon our artists than any other etcher, although Mr. Whistler is a close second. Traces of these different sources of inspiration can be detected in every Etching Club exhibition. If Mr. Whistler were a resident of his native country, he would have given a strong impetus to the development of the art. As it is, his earlier etchings of scenes along the Thames have exercised a stronger effect than his later work. Mr. Duveneck we can hardly claim as an American etcher. In quick mastery of materials and ready adaptability it would be hard to surpass our etchers; but want of originality, lack of the personal inspiration behind the executing instrument, the timidity or presumption of inexperience, and want of training—in drawing, for example—are betrayed upon the copper plate as easily as upon the canvas. There are too many openings for such criticisms in our exhibitions of etchings. But criticism is met by one fact. All this production of etchings has been evolved from nothing within a very few years. A new field has been opened in American art, and although its produce may not be perfect, its fruitfulness is better than sterility.

With the general public our etchers are faring well, but our print-collectors are beginning once more to pass by on the other side. It is true that the print-collector ordinarily concerns himself but little with the work of his own time. His luxurious dilettanteism — I use the word in no unkindly sense — has passed into a proverb. To the collectors of early engravings the history of the world begins, not perhaps with Finiguerra, but certainly with Marc Antonio Raimondi, Schöngauer, and the great Albert **Dürer.** For him the names of **Edelinck, Nanteuil,** Drevet, John George Wille, famous for his pupils as for his work, Friedrich Müller, whose memory will last until **Raphael's Sistine Madonna** is forgotten, and the Italian engravers, from Raphael Morghen **to Toschi,** interpret the history of different nations in **succeeding** generations. England **means** Sir Robert Strange, William Sharp, **and** William Woollet. The history of the world came to an end some seventy years ago, and **now,** says **the** collector, **there** is but one line-engraver living, if indeed he still lives—the German **Mandel.**[3] Mingled with his engravings the collector will have etchings, but his dreams are of **rare** states of Rembrandt, Van Ostade, Claude, Ruysdael, **Paul Potter,** Dujardin, **Van Dyck,** and other departed masters. His bible is not Hamerton, but Bartsch, which he revises himself by the aid of Passavant and Thausing, with possible occasional references to Bryan's "Dictionary of Painters and Engravers." He is in this century, but not of it. And yet the *renaissance* of etching in this generation arouses for a time the attention of the print-collector. Once in a while some event like the sale of the Claghorn collection brings into public notice the prints gathered by our amateurs, but for the most part the public is quite unconscious of these treasures.

Perhaps the late Francis C. Gray, of Boston, may be counted as "the patriarch and *facile princeps* of the tribe," to use the words of an eminent collector. Of him my informant writes: "He made a large assemblage of engravings in the early part of the century, but, although a man of great taste and general knowledge in letters as well as in art, he had not the requisite perceptions for a discriminating collector. Some forty years ago, however, he made the acquaintance of a German connoisseur, Mr. Thies, and under that gentleman's advice added to his portfolios many very fine specimens of the highest quality in etching and engraving. The whole was bequeathed at his death, about 1856, to Harvard College, after which a *catalogue raisonné* was edited by Mr. Thies. [This collection is now at the Boston Museum of Art.] The late Mr. Phillips, of Philadelphia, was a contemporary of Mr. Gray, and likewise accumulated a very large stock of prints between 1820 and 1860. I think, but am not sure, that it was he who inoculated the late

Mr. Claghorn with the chalcographic virus. At any rate, they were close friends. Mr. Phillips bequeathed his collection to the Pennsylvania Academy of Fine Arts. I spent a day in 1855 in Mr. Phillips' sanctum, looking over his things, but they betrayed rather the *cacoethes habendi* than *cavendo tutum*, which should be the motto of the true collector, for there is no end of prints." In New York, the earliest collectors were Michael Paff, John Allen, and Ithiel Town. Mr. Paff, who is still well remembered, was, in 1840, the leading dealer in prints and pictures. The engravings collected by John Allen were chiefly of the English and French schools of the seventeenth century. The catalogue of these prints, which were sold in 1864, included six hundred and thirty-eight numbers. Mr. Pickering, an American residing for some time in London, collected many good English prints, which were sold in 1826 at an auction-house in Wall Street, on the site now occupied by the Phœnix Bank. A veteran print-collector writes me: "I have further to mention the name of Robert Balmanno, very noted among English collectors. He came to America about 1829—died, in Brooklyn, in 1861. The most of his prints were sold in London in 1828, but he brought with him many fine specimens of the early masters, which were gradually disposed of during his residence here. Still another old collector of note in this city was the French Consul-General, M. de la Forest, long resident in New York, but who retired to France on the abdication of Louis Philippe, in 1848. He had many old prints, a sale of which (said, however, not to have included the choicer specimens) took place in 1849." Mr. E. L. Corwin made a large collection of prints before 1800, favoring engravings by Bartolozzi. Mr. Emil Seitz is mentioned as the first to enter upon the business of dealing in old prints in New York. When Mr. Henry F. Sewall began his rarely successful career as a collector, in 1847, he was, with the exception of a Scotchman temporarily resident here, the only American correspondent of Edward Evans, then the chief print-seller of London. The latter sent out by sailing-vessels portfolios of prints from which Mr. Sewall made his selections, thus beginning a collection chosen with singular discrimination, and now famous among print lovers. Mr. James L. Claghorn, of Philadelphia, began his collection about 1857, and I suppose brought together a larger number of prints than any other American. This collection, after futile efforts to secure it for the government or some public institution, was recently bought by Mr. T. Harrison Garrett, of Baltimore. Modern as well as early prints filled Mr. Claghorn's portfolios. Over his nearly complete set of Dr. Haden's etchings he lingered perhaps as lovingly as over his rare group of engravings by Toschi after Correggio. He owned one of the few impressions taken from the little gold plate upon which the Crucifixion was engraved by Albert Dürer to be inserted in the head of the Emperor Maximilian's favorite walking-stick. He acquired other work by the masters, but when the etchings of Delacroix, Jacque, Daubigny, and Meissonier showed a coming revival in the art, he turned to modern prints, manifesting his interest finally, I fear, with more liberality than discretion. Mr. S. P. Avery's fine collection includes not only almost unattainable proofs from plates etched by the modern French masters, but also etchings by Haden and Whistler, which neither the artists nor the British Museum possess. It was their habit to take their plates to a Paris printer, and if the first impressions were unsatisfactory, they would throw aside the proofs and re-work or perhaps destroy the plates. The printer obediently crumpled up and apparently threw away the proofs, but after the artists had gone he carefully gathered up the unique impressions, tenderly smoothed them out, and preserved them. Mr. Avery was one of the first to enter Paris after the siege, and going to this printer, he found him sitting in a room which gaped with holes made by Prussian shells, but the prints were safe, and of some Mr. Avery became the owner. When Dr. Haden visited this country he was surprised to find in Mr. Avery's collection prints of his own which he supposed were not in existence, which he certainly could not duplicate. Mr. Avery has over four hundred etchings by Jacque alone. But of print-collecting, as of prints, there is no end, and the bare mention of a few American collectors must suffice. The list is by no means exhausted with the names of Professor Charles E. West, of Brooklyn; the Honorable C. S. Bradley and Royal Taft, of Providence, R. I.; Dr. Karmann and William Henry Davis, of Cincinnati; Henry T. Field and George A. Armour, of Chicago. Messrs.

Robert Hoe, Jr., and Henry G. Marquand are among the many New York owners of prints. In this city, as in Boston, Philadelphia, and Providence, small collections are numerous, sometimes containing prints of exceptional worth.

For a time, as I have said, the print-collectors have dabbled in modern etchings, but experts testify that they are returning to the old line engravings and the etchings of the early masters. In this field the collector can secure, if not unique, at least extremely rare impressions; but hundreds of others may share his ownership of a modern etching, and amiable selfishness has much to do with print-collecting. The artistic status of these early prints is fixed. They will not be surpassed. Moreover, they can be measured by an assured standard, and their value increases every year. Here the collector feels that he has something to go upon, and we cannot blame him, since his search for prints recognized as the standards in work with the burin or needle may ultimately aid the education of our public. In modern etching, notwithstanding the enormous production, the masters have been but few. And it is this very productiveness which discourages the print-collector, and will, I think, overshoot its mark. Any demand in this age is fostered, and all the resources of active brains are taxed for its supply. The existence of a demand for etchings caused the invention of a process for steel-facing the plates by the aid of electricity. The superior resistance of steel over copper secures the printing of a larger edition. A good printer will detect the first signs of wear in the steel facing, and will substitute another, thus further increasing the edition. In some cases the original plates are electrotyped, and the printing is done entirely from the electrotypes. As regards the steel facing, it may be said that Mr. Haden, whose later plates have been steel-faced, has acknowledged that he could not tell by examining an etching whether the plate had been steel-faced or not. With intelligent printing the result is as satisfactory in one case as the other. Probably few laymen could detect prints from electrotypes. But some of the Paris publishers have injured etchings by their hasty, perfunctory, and mechanical labor to supply the market. Not many years ago Paris was deemed the only place where etchings could be satisfactorily printed, but our artists have long since willingly intrusted their plates to American printers, and much of the cheaper Paris printing is disappointing. Now, such mechanical aids as these just referred to increase the number of etchings to an extent which may be a matter for congratulation or for alarm. Moreover, there are other devices which tend in the same direction. In "typographic etching" no acid is used, but after the lines have been cut through the ground upon the plate, the untouched portions of the ground are carefully built up with wax, until the plate becomes a mould for the electrotyper. In "white line etching" the usual procedure is reversed, and the artist draws the whites in his subject on the grounded plate, leaving undisturbed the parts which will ultimately be printed, as in wood-engraving. This process, however, can hardly be regarded as worth much consideration. Mr. Amand-Durand, with the help of a Scottish artist, Mr. George Reid, has perfected a process in which the artist has nothing whatever to do with the plate. His part ends with the making of a pen-drawing on white paper. This is transferred to the grounded plate by photography. The ground is so prepared that the spaces between the lines of the drawing will be insoluble in water, while the lines themselves can be easily washed out in warm water. Then the plate is ready for biting and retouching if necessary—matters attended to by a professional engraver. Mr. Hamerton considers that "the result is just as much a real etching on copper as an original plate by Rembrandt, the essential difference being that the drawing is done on paper by one artist, and all the work on copper by another." He even finds this process superior, since a drawing in black ink on white paper shows the intended effect at once, and the artist can see it, instead of calculating it like an etcher. With all the mechanical aids which the production of etchings is receiving, it would seem that they may ere long be turned out as easily and plentifully as process-prints. A hasty pen-and-ink sketch may be magnified into thousands of etchings within a few days. Engraving deteriorated in this way even in the last generation, owing to a demand for an abundance of cheap work. There is danger, it seems to me, that this may happen to etching. It is somewhat surprising to find Mr. Hamerton eulogizing a semi-mechanical process in as high terms as he employed in describing the beauties of the line traced by the hand of the artist upon copper, and its "velvety richness" in the printing.

The demand indicated by this great output of etchings is seldom analyzed. In this country, for example, do the scores of thousands who buy etchings feel the intrinsic individuality and freedom of the etcher's line? Do they choose etchings because their eyes are educated to see the superiority of the etcher's work over that of the engraver? Does an etching appeal to them with a personal force which they do not find in a photogravure? Is it for art's sake that they take the etching, or is it for the sake of fashion? Let us be candid. The wholesale buying of etchings which has developed within the last ten years does not mean that all this army of buyers has suddenly been educated up to a point of discriminating appreciation. It does not mean that all the people who go to choose etchings with a text from Hamerton in their mouths can give intelligent reasons for their choice. Mr. Hamerton's writings have been read from the Atlantic to the Pacific, and it has dawned upon many readers that a liking for etchings is an evidence of a refined and cultivated taste. Is it not more reasonable to believe that Mr. Hamerton and other influences have popularized etchings, than that the innate intelligence of a people without special experience or knowledge in matters of art has caused this preference for the etcher's work? In other words, it has become fashionable to show an interest in and love for etchings, just as it has been the fashion to claim all sorts of beauties for any canvas bearing the names of the painters of Fontainebleau, Barbizon, and Ville d'Avray. Fickle fashion is an unreliable factor in the building up of an art, and there are signs that a reaction is close at hand. This will cause a process of elimination, resulting in the survival of the etchers who are best equipped for their work, and of the buyers who have acquired a genuine appreciation of etchings.

Mr. Frederick Keppel has kindly prepared for me a memorandum of his sales of modern etchings for a given month — March — in every year since 1875. This shows the proportion of the sales of modern etchings to the total sales, and the figures are as follows:

1875.....2 per cent.	1880.....15 per cent.
1876.....2 "	1881.....26 "
1877.....9½ "	1882.....33 "
1878.....21 "	1883.....73 "
1879.....9 "	

In March, 1884, the percentage fell to sixty per cent., and in 1885 was nearly the same, or sixty-two per cent. The striking increase from two per cent., in 1875, to 73 per cent., in 1883, certainly suggests the question whether such a rapid gain can be permanent. Mr. Keppel writes: "The figures for the whole year would probably alter these somewhat, but as they are they show pretty well what etchings have been doing in the last ten years. Though etchings are still sought for by many buyers, there is certainly an increasing demand for fine engravings; at least we find it so here." I have no doubt that Messrs. Wunderlich, Buonaventure, and other printsellers would tell a similar story. They would probably confirm Mr. Keppel's testimony that the print-collectors on the one hand are going back to early engravings and etchings, and that the popular demand is slowly abating. An eminent etcher has said to me: "The craze for etchings is like the craze for roller-skating. It will pass away." His expression admits of some modification. People who simply want pictures at a smaller cost than oil-paintings are apt to demand "as much of a picture as possible for their money." To them a freely-drawn sketch of a Thames scene by Whistler is not "enough of a picture." They look for something which will make a better showing on their walls. Out of twenty men, nineteen will admire mechanical excellence, nicety of finish, for one who will appreciate artistic feeling. And yet this does not mean the downfall of etching, but it does suggest the necessity of confining etching to its own appropriate and individual rôle.

This popular demand for elaboration has already injured etching by blurring its distinctive character. Is it not true that, as regards the popular methods of etching, the pendulum is swinging back to the engraver-etching, which alone represented the art in the past? In the early days of the modern revival, Mr. Hamerton fixed a standard based upon the work of the great etchers. He wrote: "To feel vividly, to be possessed for a few hours by some overmastering thought, and record the thought before the fire has time to die out of it, this is the first condition of success in etching." Mr. Haden said: "The point must be the voice that ever runs ahead of the art inspiration, recording the heat of passionate inspiration." It was as a direct autographic expression in linear form that we were taught to prize the etching; but what a change has come even in this short time! In England, the places of honor are accorded to the etchings of Frederick Slocombe, R. W. Macbeth, M. S. Menpes, C. O. Murray, and others in whose hands the autographic treatment of lines is replaced by attempts at elaborate gradations of tones, aided by the use of the burin, roller, scraper, and of retroussage or any help that the printer can give. Such efforts at tonality and the attainment of all the values possible in the range between black and white, appear even in Mr. Hamerton's own journal, *The Portfolio*, with his endorsement. If Mr. Hamerton has been converted to the doctrine of elaboration, the art of etching is sadly in need of a new evangelist. Mr. Haden's "passionate inspiration" is at present expended upon mezzo-tints. In France, professional reproductive etching has far outstripped the freer work of painter-etchers. Among the followers of Flameng, a score or more might be named who send us engraver-etchings executed with wonderful skill and subtlety, but this is not the kind of achievement that made the school of Rembrandt immortal. In our own Etching Club Exhibitions, Mr. Farrer's careful attention to tonality, and some examples by Messrs. Hamilton Hamilton, Thomas Hovenden, J. S. King, Benjamin Lander, and others, have shown the same tendency to elaboration. In reproductive etching this is expected to a certain extent; but Mr. Hamerton, although his profession of faith is hardly borne out by his subsequent practices, has shown the danger of attempted imitation of "the minute intermediate tones attained in true chiaroscuro methods," and has warned etchers to "suggest" tones which cannot be given accurately, instead of "laboriously trying to imitate paintings tone by tone."

The tendency toward elaborate work is not confined to reproductive etching, but I think that the etchers make a mistake who endeavor to attract the public by a high degree of mechanical excellence. For they not only enter the field of the engraver, but they place themselves in competition with photography as employed in the printing-press. There are processes, especially those associated with the names Amand-Durand and Goupil, which are likely to take a strong hold upon the public fancy. I have seen a reproduction by Amand-Durand of a print by Albert Dürer, the exactitude of which was wonderful, and this process is to be employed, I believe, in the republication of rare prints contemplated by the Chalcographical Society. Take some of the plates recently published by Messrs. Boussod, Valadon & Co., of Paris, and note the development of the Goupil photo-engraving process and its combination with the etching-needle until the result, an English writer says, "has almost as good a right to be called an etching as a photo-gravure." The brain impulse, which should be behind the etcher's line, is too precious to be wasted in working and re-working a plate into a semblance of a photo-engraving. Etching is not an imitative art, for there are no lines in nature and the etching line is conventional. But it is suggestive, and this is enough. Mr. Haden has said: "The properties of the etching line are almost wholly mental, consisting of personality, actuality, and originality. We can recognize the line of Rembrandt or Claude." Could we recognize an individual artist's line in some of the popular modern etchings? Now American etching has produced a surprising quantity of good work, and some much more than good, within a very short time. The faithful labor and creditable achievements of our etchers must be recognized by every student of the subject. On the other hand, it must be acknowledged that if our etchers are to make themselves felt as artists, they must avoid certain tendencies of the present day. In all art, simplicity is best. An etching which may be popularly termed "only a sketch," may show not only more vital energy, but far more profound knowledge than another finished like an engraving. Only a master of his art can venture upon the sketchy manner which so often tempts ignorance into self-betrayal. The painter-etcher knows that tact in omission is a test of his understanding of his art, and omissions may reveal more peculiar aptness than the treatment of parts presented in the composition. If etching is to be confounded with semi-mechanical methods of reproduction, the modern revival will have occurred in vain. But the path for our artists to follow seems to me sufficiently clear. They must go back to etching as it was practised by the masters; as Mr. Hamerton explained it in his earlier writings. They must invest etching with a distinct individual character, not attempting to make it more than it is, not consenting to lower its intrinsic worth. The time has come when our people wish to see for themselves in etchings the precise merits which they have taken on faith from Mr. Hamerton. It rests with our artists to maintain the rank of pure etching. The fashion of admiring etchings may pass, but, like all such fancies, it will leave much good behind. It has taught many to study etchings carefully, and thus insured a permanent and intelligent, if smaller, audience for our etchers. The number of etchers may diminish with the ebbing of the popular tide; but the strongest, who remain, will be put upon their mettle, and even if the number of American etchings decreases, I think that a cultivated taste may find sufficient consolation in improved quality for any falling off in quantity. If American etching shall come to be recognized as creative work, distinguished by its simplicity of expression, its forcefulness of execution, and its distinct personal element, we may be sure that the art will receive a rational appreciation.

These generalities can be readily illustrated. Twenty years ago, and less, the public demand for prints was satisfied with steel engravings. It is now nearly ten years since the steel engraving was sent to keep company with black-walnut, horse-hair furniture and white-marble mantels. Here is one advance, due partly, as I have indicated, to fashion, and partly, also, to a real perception of the superior freedom of the etcher's work and the superior softness and richness of the line etched upon copper. At first there was a general preference for the etchings which, in workmanship, most closely resembled the old steel engraving, like the etchings of the late A. F. Bellows. But just as the print-collectors, who began by acquiring every new etching, were soon forced by the great production to pause, and to substitute careful selection for wholesale acquisition, so a certain portion of the public has learned to exercise intelligent discrimination in the choice of etchings, and there is the testimony of the print-sellers that the number of these has greatly increased within the last six years. And with the increase of a class who prefer expressive simplicity to the elaboration of the etcher, who "tells all he knows" at tedious length, and who look for imagination and suggestiveness instead of facts and details, the etcher will feel the growing pressure of a healthier stimulus. From this, and from the competition of purely mechanical work, there may come a process of elimination resulting in the survival of the fittest etchers; or, at least, the line will become more sharply drawn, more apparent to the public.

But there is a limit to the development of public taste. The painter-etching, which connoisseurs and collectors prize for certain subtle qualities of line or light and shade, is usually less interesting to the public, and this, I think, will always be the case. But, granting this, it is not necessary to fall back upon the merely "pictorial" or "decorative" style of etching which, within the last three years, has been too much in vogue. Much of this is "painter-etching," technically considered, for the artist has etched his own picture. Few members of the New York Etching Club have done any reproductive etching of consequence, and reproductive etchers are still, of course, in a minority, although the amount of reproductive work has increased so much that it has gained a distinct place in American etching. And it goes without saying that reproductive etching has its place everywhere. But all "painter-etching" is not pure etching, nor fairly representative of the art, and those who do not go beyond this term must expect plenty of "pretty" subjects treated in a "pictorial" and, it may be added, a commercial way. Happily, some American artists furnish excellent illustrations of pure etching which are within the reach of every one. Their subjects in themselves are not uninteresting, and their methods are for the most part appropriate.

Mr. Whistler's etchings, despite his real eminence, and, shall I say, his notoriety, still appeal to connoisseurs rather than to our public. But, looking over some portfolios of etchings before me, I find work by American members of what may be termed the school of Whistler, Messrs. Duveneck, Pennell, and Bacher, which will interest both the connoisseur and the public. Now, Mr. Whistler's etchings offer one of the best possible illustrations of the art of expressing much with apparently slight means, of true suggestiveness, and his figures in his best work have a distinctly human significance, which is one of the artist's individual successes. Here, to leave Mr. Whistler, who is American only by the accident of birth, both Messrs. Duveneck and Bacher fail. Their figures are often wraith-like, impersonal, unmeaning incidents of architectural studies or waterscapes, and this is especially disappointing in Mr. Bacher's etchings, because figures form no inconsiderable part of his compositions. Mr. Duveneck deals in contrasts, suggesting much, never aiming at delicate tonic gradations. As examples of not unpopular subjects treated in a free, autographic manner, yet with pictorial concessions, I may instance two of his most recent etchings: first, "Desdemona's House, Venice;" and, second, "The Rialto." As embodying simplicity of method, and sufficiency and harmony of effect, there is Mr. Bacher's "The Lido, Venice," with his "Entrance to the Grand Canal, Venice," which shows some of his happiest architectural work. Next come some impressions which will do more than any printed arguments to shed light upon that much vexed question of "adventitious aid" in printing. Here is Mr. Bacher's "Lustheim," printed with and without *retroussage;* that is, the dragging of the ink out of the intaglio lines in the plate by means of a soft rag passed lightly over them. The etching, simply printed, is an outline drawing, which will be deemed a skeleton by one who asks something more than purely linear effects. With *retroussage* the bones are clothed with flesh, and an impression is produced far richer and fuller than before. With these impressions is Mr. Bacher's "Rainy Night, Venice," printed from a plate wiped with a dry rag, which has spread the ink along the sides of the lines without bringing them together as in *retroussage*, thus producing a sombre evenness of tone. Now, the question of how far the etcher is justified in seeking aid from the printer is one upon which I do not propose to enter. Neither do I deem it necessary to renew discussion of the "limitations" of etching, for it seems to me that the intelligently directed study of such representative etchings as are contained in the portfolio before me will be more profitable than the acceptance of any dicta. Take some of Mr. Pennell's etchings, "The Landing Place, Leghorn," and "The Swing of the Arno," and note the support gained for his lines by his course in stopping out his whites and attacking the copper directly with acid, or by removing enough of the ground with sand-paper to permit a slight corrosion of the plate. These means are of course quite outside of simple draughtmanship with the needle, and yet these and others of a similar kind have been employed since the history of etching began; and their admissibility or value can be decided by anyone for himself with the etchings in question before him. Not so much for this, however, as for the free, bold sweep of lines, are these etchings worth attention, and the same linear beauty appears in some of Mr. Pennell's etchings of bridges over the Arno, a beauty forming no slight feature of Méryon's "Apse of Nôtre Dame," and "Pont au Change." In the "Archway, Pistoria," and in various Florentine studies, Mr. Pennell's vivacious touch is seen to even better advantage. We may quarrel with his mannerisms, and his overbitten opaque shadows, or what not, but, after all, his work is stimulating and interesting.

There is another "school" in this country, according to foreign critics—

the "school of Seymour Haden"—and among its pupils Messrs. Platt and Parrish are assigned a leading place. Of Mr. Platt's earlier, and perhaps fresher, work I can point out no better example than " The Market Slip, Low Tide, St. John, N. B." Once in a European capital this etching was received with incredulity by a company of eminent connoisseurs. And when convinced of its American origin, an Italian collector said: "I knew that pork and petroleum came from America. I did not know that America produced works of art like this." Since then foreign amateurs have found reasons for couching their compliments to our etchers in more graceful terms. Mr. Platt's "Low Tide" is notable for the excellent composition of which the fine confusion of masts and rigging to the left forms a striking part, for the easy yet assured tracing of lines against the sky, for the suggestive dampness of the foreground, and for the atmospheric effect, the light streaming out from the horizon, an effect very materially aided by the printing. Less strong, but yet extremely good, is an example of Mr. Platt's recent work, "On the Connecticut River," a sloop beside an old wharf, and a far-reaching stretch of water, with buildings on the shore; a simple composition, but valuable for this reason, among others, that the etcher has not allowed himself to do too much. Of Mr. Parrish's recent work there is no better example than his large etching of "London Bridge." The crowded shipping of the Thames and its eddying waters have been treated by master-hands before, but in his drawing and his avoidance of undue detail Mr. Parrish has acquitted himself well. His composition loses something in directness through the abundance of its elements, but one will be long in exhausting the fine points of this etching. Nothing that Mr. Parrish has done, however, seems to me more vigorous than his "Low Tide, Bay of Fundy," with the strong lines of stranded vessels outstanding against a brilliant sky, balanced by quaint houses on the shore, and with another touch added in the expressive figures on the beach. This is perhaps the only American etching which has been purchased for one of the great Continental collections, that at Vienna, of which Adam Bartsch was the curator seventy years ago. These etchings surely have a sufficiently pictorial value, but one who emphasizes this aspect of the etching may perhaps find greater satisfaction in Mr. Peter Moran's "Passing Storm," and "A New England Orchard." In one, cattle pace leisurely over a sunny, finely-rendered foreground, while behind them comes the sombre march of bursting rain-clouds. Something might be said against the heaviness of the down-pouring sheets of rain, but this is a matter to be settled between the etcher and his printer. Very different is the orchard scene, glittering with sunlight, where a flock of sheep graze beneath the apple-boughs. This is worth study as an example of tact in omission. The etcher has carried his work far enough; he has not enfeebled his plate by over-elaboration. And yet his method of expression is very different from that of Mrs. M. Nimmo Moran, whose "Goosepond" and "Summer at East Hampton" may be taken as excellent examples of vigorous line-work. As stimuli of the imagination I may take Mr. Thomas Moran's study of a breaking wave, called "The Sounding Sea," provoking yet interesting, and his mysterious "Twilight in Arizona," the latter exemplifying the use of the *roulette*, and not the autographic drawing which is the peculiar charm of etching. But this is one of the many resources of the etcher, like the artificial printing of Miss E. L. Peirce's admirably sympathetic "Road to the Beach." Here, at least, I think the printer must share with the etcher the honors of a plate which simply printed would have obtained a far less degree of popular success.

These examples are enough, perhaps, for my purpose, which has been only to point out, without detailed discussion, some American painter-etchings which are accessible at most print-shops of consequence, which possess intrinsic artistic merit, which illustrate the scope and versatility of the etcher's resources, and which, with few exceptions, are pure etchings. I am well aware that the landscapes and Venetian scenes of Mr. Gifford, such etchings as Mr. Van Elten's "Holland Wind-Mill" and "In the Meadows," the landscapes of Messrs. Smillie, Farrer, Yale, and the excellent work of other etchers, will be suggested to many possibly with equal force; but, as I have said, it is impossible in these limits to analyze the work of all American etchers. What I have aimed to do is to supplement enforced generalities with such pertinent and convenient illustrations that my readers may be helped to a practical and intelligent study of etching in America. Etchings like those which I have cited are not to be held lightly by the most refined connoisseur, while on the other hand they contain enough pictorial incident and charm of subject to satisfy a want which cannot be altogether ignored. Since they show the true application of the art, there is much to be learned from them. It is fortunate that we have at hand such instructive teachers of the public. Elsewhere I have deplored certain inartistic commercial tendencies which have been making themselves felt in our etching, but I would not be thought to fail in recognizing the persistence of tendencies in the right direction. No one who cares a straw for art can fail to honor our best painter-etchers for their admirable achievements, and the veriest Gradgrind may well be moved by the noble recognition accorded them abroad. The recent past of etching in America is more than creditable. Its present, despite signs of immaturity and commercialism, offers many reasons for hopefulness. Its future standing depends upon the maintenance by our etchers of etching as an art.

AMERICAN ETCHERS.

THIS list, including, as it does, the names of nearly all the artists who have exhibited with the New York Etching Club, contains the names of many whose work with the needle is intermittent and incidental. On the other hand, a few artists who exhibited with the club in its earlier years have been omitted, because they appear to have abandoned entirely this branch of art.

* *Member New York Etching Club.*
† *Member* Society Painter-Etchers, London.

ADAMS, J. WOOD,	New York.
†BACHER, OTTO H.,	Cleveland, O.
*BALDWIN, A. H.,	New York.
BAUER, W. C.,	Elizabeth, N. J.
BICKNELL, A. H.,	Malden, Mass.
BLUM, ROBERT,	New York.
CALAHAN, JAMES J.,	New York.
CHAMPNEY, J. WELLS,	" "
CHASE, HARRY,	" "

*Chase, W. M., ... New York.
*†Church, F. S., . . . " "
  Clements, Gabrielle D., Philadelphia, Pa.
  Cole, J. Foxcroft, . . Boston, Mass.
*Colman, Samuel, . . Newport, R. I.
  Corwin, Charles.

  Daingerfield, Elliott, . . New York.
  De Haas, M. F. H., . . " "
*Dielman, Frederick, . . " "
  Dillaye, Blanche, . . Philadelphia, Pa.
  Dixwell, Anna P., . . Boston, Mass.
  Dougherty, Parke C., . Philadelphia, Pa.
†Duveneck, Frank.

  Earle, L. C., ... Chicago, Ill.
  Ehninger, John W., . Saratoga, N. Y.
*Eno, Henry C., . . . New York.

*†Falconer, J. M., . . Brooklyn, N. Y.
*†Farrer, Henry, . . . New York.
  Ferris, Gerome, . . Philadelphia, Pa.
  Ferris, S. J. . . . " "

  Garrett, Edmund H., . Boston, Mass.
*Gaugengigl, I. M., . . . " "
*†Gifford, R. Swain, . . . New York.

Greatorex, Eliza,	New York.
Guy, S. J.,	" "
Hamilton, Hamilton,	New York.
Heinicke, Otto,	" "
Hill, J. Henry,	Mont Moor, N. Y.
Hovenden, Thomas,	Plymouth Meeting, Pa.
Hunter, F. Leo,	Cold Spring, N. Y.
Jones, Alfred,	New York.
Juengling, Fred.,	" "
King, James S.,	New York.
Lander, Benjamin,	New York.
Lauber, Joseph,	" "
Le Fevre, W. J.,	Philadelphia, Pa.
Lesley, Margaret W.,	" "
Levin, Katherine,	" "
Lovewell, R.	Chelsea, Mass.
Low, Will. H.,	New York.
Mansfield, John W.,	New York.
Martin, T. M.,	" "
Matlack, Eleanor,	Philadelphia, Pa.
Mielatz, C. F. W.,	Newport, R. I.
*Miller, C. H.,	New York.

Miller, E. F.,	Columbus, O.
Miller, E. H.,	Washington, D. C.
Mills, Charles E.,	Pittsburg, Pa.
Millspaugh, J. H.,	Jersey City, N. J.
*Monks, J. A. S.,	New York.
Moran, Emily,	Philadelphia, Pa.
*†Moran, M. Nimmo,	New York.
*Moran, Peter,	Philadelphia, Pa.
*†Moran, Thomas,	New York.
Neely, J., Jr.,	Philadelphia, Pa.
*Nicoll, J. C.,	New York.
*†**Parrish, Stephen,**	Philadelphia, Pa.
Peirce, **Edith Loring,**	" "
*†Pennell, Joseph,	" "
*†Platt, C. A.,	New York.
*Reinhart, C. S.,	New York.
Richards, F. De B.,	Philadelphia, Pa.
Ritchie, G. W. H.,	New York.
*Robbins, H. W.,	" "
*Sabin, J. F.,	New York.
*Sartain, William,	" "
*Satterlee, Walter,	" "
Schilling, Alexander,	Chicago, Ill.

Schoff, S. A.,	Boston, Mass.
Sewell, R. V. V.,	New York.
Share, H. P.,	" "
Shelton, W. H.,	" "
*Shirlaw, Walter,	" "
*Smillie, George H.,	" "
*†Smillie, James D.,	" "
*Twachtman, J. H.,	Cincinnati, O.
Twachtman, Mrs. J. H.,	" "
Vanderhoff, Charles A.,	New York.
*†Van Elten, Kruseman,	" "
Volkmar, Charles,	" "
Walker, Horatio,	Rochester, N. Y.
Wallace, W. H.,	Brooklyn, N. Y.
Waller, Frank,	New York.
†Whistler, James McNeil,	London, England.
Whittemore, C. E.,	New York.
Whittemore, W. J.,	" "
Wiseman, Robert R.,	New Haven, Conn.
*Wood, T. W.,	New York.
*Yale, L. M.,	New York.
Yewell, G. H.,	" "

AMERICAN PRINT-COLLECTORS AND PUBLIC COLLECTIONS.

ARMOUR, GEORGE A., Chicago, Ill., *old engravings and etchings.*

AVERY, S. P., New York, *Haden, Whistler,* **and** *modern French etchings.*

BATES, ISAAC C., *old line-engraved portraits.*

BOSTON MUSEUM OF FINE ARTS, Boston, Mass., *American etchings and other prints.*

BRADLEY, C. S., Providence, R. I., *school of Dürer, etc.*

CLAGHORN COLLECTION, owned by T. HARRISON GARRETT, Baltimore, Md., *some twenty thousand old and modern prints.*

DAVIS, WILLIAM HENRY, Cincinnati, O., *line-engravings.*

FIELD, HENRY T., Chicago, Ill., *modern etchings.*

GRAY COLLECTION, owned by Harvard University, at present in the Boston Museum of Fine Arts, *six thousand old prints.*

GRIGGS, L. D., New York, *old prints.*

HAMILL, CHARLES D., Chicago, Ill., *Rembrandt and his school.*

HOE, ROBERT, New York, *Dürer, etc.*

IRWIN, THEODORE, Oswego, N. Y., *fine examples of Rembrandt, Dürer, etc.*

KARMANN, DR., Cincinnati, O.

KING COLLECTION, Redwood Library, Newport, R. I., *old English, Italian, and Dutch engravings.*

LEA, HENRY C., Philadelphia, Pa., *Van Dyck Iconography, portraits with outlines etched by Van Dyck.*

MANSFIELD, HOWARD, New York, *fine modern etchings.*

MARSH COLLECTION, Smithsonian Institute, Washington, D. C., *old line-engravings.*

MARQUAND, HENRY G., New York.

PHILLIPS COLLECTION, Pennsylvania Academy of Fine Arts, *sixty thousand prints, historically most valuable.*

ROGERS, EDMUND LAW, Baltimore, Md., *old line-engravings.*

SEWELL, HENRY F., New York, *eighteen thousand old prints, representing the best work of engravers and etchers.*

TAFT, ROYAL, Providence, R. I., *rare proofs of pure line-engravings.*

TOSTI COLLECTION, Boston Public Library, *six thousand old engravings.*

WEST, PROFESSOR CHARLES E., Brooklyn, N. Y., *fine old prints.*

YOUNG MEN'S CHRISTIAN ASSOCIATION, New York, *eight thousand engraved portraits.*

NOTES.

1. (Page 19.) Mr. Smillie died in December, 1885.

2. (Page 35.) Mr. Gifford published etchings as early as 1865 or 1866, and Dr. Yale, with Mr. James D. Smillie and a few others, etched some plates about that time.

3. (Page 44.) Mandel is not living.

NEW ART PUBLICATIONS.

ETCHINGS.

Every copy of SOME MODERN ETCHINGS *having been sold by the publishers, unsigned impressions of the etched plates are now offered separately or as a set* WITHOUT TEXT, *as follows:* Each etching neatly matted. TESTING THE TOLEDO, *by Frank Waller*—MY AIN FIRESIDE, *by S. G. McCutcheon*—A TRAMP, *by Gabrielle D. Clements*—PORTRAIT OF REMBRANDT, *by J. S. King*—PONTE SAN TRINITA, *by Joseph Pennell*—THE EVENING STAR, *by Walter Satterlee*—NEVER TOO LATE TO MEND, *by J. Wells Champney*—DRIVING SHEEP, *by J. A. S. Monks*—AN OLD MASTER AT LAST, *by Elliott Dangerfield*—CLARIONET PLAYER, *by Katherine Levin.*

Impressions on Japan paper, each $2.50; the set of ten in neat portfolio, $20.00.

THE CHRISTIAN UNION says: "CLARA ERSKINE CLEMENT has supplemented her well-known and admirable 'History of Painting' by a new volume, published in the same style, and containing *An Outline History of*

SCULPTURE FOR BEGINNERS AND STUDENTS."

Of this work THE BOSTON ADVERTISER says: "The author has given to her text almost the fascination of a well-told story."

THE BOSTON BEACON says: "It may heartily be recommended as thoroughly sound, accurate and helpful."

Fully and handsomely illustrated with 122 *full-page illustrations or cuts set in the text. With complete indexes.*

8vo. Tastefully bound. With artistic designs stamped in gold on cloth covers, $2.50. Half calf, $4.50.

Covers the ground in an interesting way, giving a good idea of all the great sculptors and their works, as well as enabling any one who wishes a general knowledge of the subject to obtain it in a pleasant way. Very readable.

New catalogue with full descriptions of many interesting art publications mailed free to any address, on application.

Any of the above can be had of your bookseller, or will be sent to any address, at publishers' expense, on receipt of advertised price.

WHITE, STOKES, & ALLEN,
PUBLISHERS,
182 FIFTH AVENUE, NEW YORK CITY.

www.ingramcontent.com/pod-product-compliance
Lightning Source LLC
Chambersburg PA
CBHW021946160426
43195CB00011B/1238